7199

19.00

THE
SAMOYED

by Charlotte Wilcox

Consultant:
Connie Rudd
Vice President
Organization for the Working Samoyed

CAPSTONE
HIGH/LOW BOOKS
an imprint of Capstone Press
Mankato, Minnesota

Capstone High/Low Books are published by Capstone Press
818 North Willow Street, Mankato, Minnesota 56001
http://www.capstone-press.com

Library of Congress Cataloging-in-Publication Data
Wilcox, Charlotte.
     The Samoyed/by Charlotte Wilcox.
     p. cm.—(Learning about dogs)
     Includes bibliographical references (p. 45) and index.
     Summary: Introduces the history, development, uses, and care of this
white dog from the far North.
     ISBN 0-7368-0161-8
     1. Samoyed dog—Juvenile literature. [1. Samoyed dog. 2. Dogs] I. Title
II. Series: Wilcox, Charlotte. Learning about dogs.
SF429.S35W55   1999
636.73—dc21   98-37634
                                                                             CIP
                                                                             AC

Editorial Credits
Timothy Halldin, cover designer; Sheri Gosewisch and Kimberly Danger, photo
     researchers

Photo Credits
Archive Photos, 27, 28
Betty Crowell, 30
Kent and Donna Dannen, cover, 4, 6, 10, 13, 17, 18, 23, 24, 35, 36, 39, 40-41
Photri-Microstock/Gunvor Jørgsholm, 9, 20
Visuals Unlimited, 32; Visuals Unlimited/N. Pecnik, 14

Table of Contents

Quick Facts about the Samoyed 4

Chapter 1 Snow Dogs 7

Chapter 2 The Beginnings of the Breed 15

Chapter 3 Sledding and Exploring 21

Chapter 4 The Samoyed Today 31

Chapter 5 Owning a Samoyed 37

Photo Diagram 40

Quick Facts about Dogs 42

Words to Know 44

To Learn More 45

Useful Addresses 46

Internet Sites 47

Index 48

19.00

Quick Facts about the Samoyed

Description

Height: Male Samoyeds stand 21 to 23.5 inches (53 to 60 centimeters) tall. Females stand 19 to 21 inches (48 to 53 centimeters) tall. Height is measured from the ground to the withers. The withers are the tops of the shoulders.

Weight: Male Samoyeds weigh 45 to 65 pounds (20 to 29 kilograms). Females weigh 35 to 50 pounds (16 to 23 kilograms).

Physical features: The Samoyed is medium in size. It has powerful legs and shoulders. The Samoyed's hair is straight and very thick. The Samoyed has dark eyes and pointed ears. Its long, hairy tail curls over its back.

Color: The Samoyed is pure white, cream, or biscuit. Biscuit is a very light tan.

Development

Place of origin: Samoyeds came from the Arctic in northern Asia. This area is now the country of Russia.

History of breed: People used Samoyeds to herd reindeer and pull sleds.

Numbers: The American Kennel Club registers about 4,000 Samoyeds every year in the United States. Register means to record a dog's breeding record with an official club. Canadians register about 400 Samoyeds each year.

Uses

Most Samoyeds in North America are pets. Some Samoyeds are racing sled dogs. Other Samoyeds can herd livestock.

Chapter 1
Snow Dogs

Samoyeds (sa-muh-YEDZ) have thick, fluffy hair. Samoyeds that live in cold, snowy climates roll and play in the snow. But these dogs once needed their hair to survive in a terribly cold land.

Samoyed dogs are from the continent of Asia. They came from a region 500 miles (805 kilometers) north of the Arctic Circle. The area Samoyeds came from is now called northwest Siberia. Siberia is in Russia. This area is frozen most of the year. Some features of these dogs come from being raised in this harsh climate.

Samoyed dogs originally came from a very cold climate.

Climate in the North

The land in northwest Siberia is called tundra. The winters are long and cold. The summers are short and cool. Temperatures can range from -25 degrees Fahrenheit (-32 degrees Celsius) in the winter to 40 degrees Fahrenheit (4 degrees Celsius) in the summer. Crops will grow in this harsh climate only two months each year. Summers are so short that the ground stays frozen nearly all year. Only the surface thaws in summer.

The weather affects the plants, animals, and people that live in the tundra. There are no trees. Large plants need deep soil to grow. Plants also need much water. The tundra receives less than 15 inches (38 centimeters) of rain and snow each year. Only small plants that grow close to the ground can live there. Mosses and lichens are the most common types of plant. Lichen is a flat, mosslike growth on rocks and trees.

The people and animals that live in the tundra must adapt to the harsh conditions.

People often use dogs to pull sleds in far northern lands such as the Arctic.

Small plants provide food for reindeer, arctic hares, and other arctic animals. People who live in the tundra depend on these arctic animals for food. They use animal skins for clothing.

The Samoyed people live in Siberia. Europeans named Samoyed dogs for these people. The Samoyed people first raised these

dogs. Samoyed is a Russian word. It means "people able to live by themselves."

The Samoyed people are nomads. Nomad groups face many difficulties. They care for themselves in harsh conditions. They do not live in one place all year. They travel often to find a steady supply of food. The dogs of the Samoyed people move with them. The Samoyed people depend on their dogs. The dogs are well adapted to the tundra.

Samoyed Dogs in the North

Samoyed dogs have many features that help them live in the Arctic. They have thick, warm hair. Samoyeds can survive in very cold weather. Their tails help them in the cold. Their long, curved tails have thick hair. The dogs cover their noses with their tails when they sleep. The dogs can become ill if they breathe cold air.

Other features help Samoyeds in snowy conditions. These dogs have dark brown eyes

Samoyed dogs cover their noses with their long, curved tails when they sleep.

and black eyelids. Dark colors protect their eyes from the sun's glare off the snow.

Samoyeds have special features on their feet. Their toes spread wide apart. This keeps them from sinking into deep snow when they walk. Long hairs between their toes protect their feet. Ice cannot build up and hurt their toes. The hair between their toes helps dogs on the ice. They do not slip and fall. This is important when they travel.

Samoyed dogs are strong and have great endurance. Samoyeds can work long hours and travel long distances. They do not tire easily. These features help them pull sleds through the snow.

Samoyeds also have a herding instinct. An instinct is a behavior that animals do naturally. An instinct is not learned. Hunting dogs chase birds by instinct. Herding dogs round up animals by instinct. Some Samoyed dogs have a herding instinct. Samoyed people in Siberia train their dogs to herd.

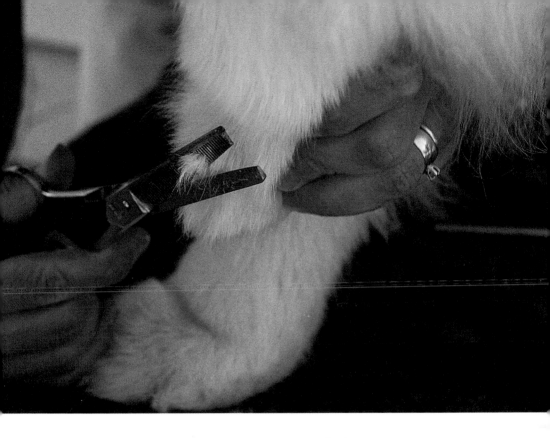

Samoyeds have long hairs between their toes to help them walk on ice.

Samoyeds are friendly dogs. They are loyal and get along well with humans. The Samoyed people treat their dogs like members of the family. Samoyed dogs are helpful and brave. At times, Samoyed dogs even have saved their owners' lives.

Chapter 2
The Beginnings of the Breed

The Samoyed people have lived in the Arctic for centuries. Some people who study history think that the Samoyed people have been there since 1000 B.C. The Samoyed people bred and raised dogs. These dogs helped the Samoyed people survive.

The Samoyed people were a self-sufficient nomad group. No other people lived near them. They were able to provide food and protection for their families. But the Samoyed people had to find food from the land around

Samoyed dogs were bred and raised in the Arctic by the Samoyed people.

them. Sometimes the Samoyed people hunted or fished. But they could not always find animals and fish. The Samoyed people needed a steady food supply.

The Samoyed people tamed herds of reindeer. The reindeer provided food for the Samoyed people. The reindeer had to move to find enough food to eat. They ate the small lichens and mosses that grow in the summer. The Samoyed people and their dogs followed the reindeer.

The Special White Dogs

The Samoyed people greatly valued their dogs. These dogs did many jobs. Teams of Samoyed dogs pulled loaded sleds through the snow. The dogs traveled long distances without becoming tired. They helped people hunt animals for food. The Samoyed dogs protected the reindeer herds. They guarded homes and villages.

The Samoyed dogs were not just good workers. The dogs were also loyal companions. They were members of the

Teams of Samoyed dogs still pull sleds through the snow today.

family. Dogs always slept inside their owners' tents at night. They would sometimes sleep under people's blankets. This kept the children warm.

The appearance of the Samoyed dog has not changed for many centuries. The Samoyed people's name for these dogs was Bjelkier (BYEL-kyur). This means "white dog that breeds white." Samoyed dogs passed on light coloring to all their puppies. They were almost

17

Samoyed dogs pass on their white coloring to their puppies.

always white or very light tan. Some
Samoyeds had light-colored fur with
black patches.

Dependent on Reindeer

Reindeer were important to the Samoyed
people's way of life. The Samoyed people bred
herds of reindeer. Reindeer provided milk and
meat for the Samoyed. The Samoyed wore

clothing made of thick reindeer fur and leather. They made their tents of reindeer skins. They also trained reindeer to pull sleds.

Reindeer eat a special plant called reindeer moss. Reindeer moss is a lichen that takes years to grow big enough for reindeer to eat. Reindeer must move often to find enough reindeer moss to survive.

The Samoyed people did not have fences for their reindeer. The reindeer needed to be free to find food to eat. Samoyed people taught their dogs to herd the reindeer. The reindeer could not run away from the Samoyed dogs. The dogs kept the baby animals with their mothers. The Samoyed dogs also protected the herd from wild animals. The survival of the reindeer was necessary. The Samoyed people depended on the reindeer to live.

Chapter 3
Sledding and Exploring

Explorers from Moscow met the Samoyed people and their dogs in the 1600s. This was the first time Europeans had seen these dogs. The explorers learned about the unusual white dogs. They sent some of these dogs to the czar (ZAR) of Russia. The czar was the ruler of Russia. The ruler's family loved the beautiful Samoyed dogs.

Czar Nicholas II was the ruler of Russia in the late 1800s. He knew that these arctic dogs pulled sleds well. The czar thought the dogs could help him.

Arctic explorers needed sled dogs like those used by native peoples in the far north.

Government workers in Russia traveled long distances between cities. The czar hired a man named Alexander Trontheim (TRON-time) to bring him more of the arctic dogs. Trontheim went to the Samoyed people and bought many dogs. Soon Samoyeds pulled sleds for government workers all across Russia.

Samoyeds in England

Ernest Kilburn-Scott loved animals. He worked for a zoo in England. He traveled to northern Russia in 1889 and brought home a puppy named Sabarka (suh-BAR-kuh). Sabarka was the first dog of its breed in England. English people called the breed Bjelkier at first. This was the Russian name for the dogs.

Kilburn-Scott wanted to know more about the dogs. He talked to people from Russia. He learned about the Samoyed people. He found out how to say and spell their name. He decided to re-name the dog breed after the Samoyed people.

Most of today's Samoyeds are related to Samoyeds that were used as sled dogs.

Kilburn-Scott started the Samoyed Club of England in 1909. Samoyeds became popular dogs in England. People in England and North America brought other dogs from Russia.

Kilburn-Scott raised many Samoyeds. He later bought more Samoyeds from polar explorers when they returned from trips. These sled dogs were the strongest and sturdiest of their breed. Most of today's Samoyeds are related to these dogs.

Samoyeds are suited to hard work and cold climates.

In 1917, the Russian Revolution took place. The government of Czar Nicholas II was overthrown. Many laws changed in Russia at this time. People from Europe and North America were not allowed to visit in Russia anymore. People could no longer buy dogs directly from the Samoyed people. People had to rely on Kilburn-Scott's dogs for breeding Samoyeds to buy and sell.

Traveling with Nansen

Fridtjof Nansen (FREED-yof NAHN-suhn) was a famous explorer from Norway. Nansen explored many places in the Arctic. He wanted to reach the North Pole. The North Pole is the point farthest north on the earth. Nansen needed to use the best sled dogs to explore the North Pole.

Nansen studied all the well-known sled-dog breeds. He learned that some sled dogs were hard to control. He learned that Samoyeds were easier to manage. Nansen decided Samoyeds would be the best dogs for his work. He bought some Samoyeds in 1893.

The journey to the North Pole was difficult. Nansen and his fellow explorer Hjalmar Johansen (HYAL-mar YOH-hahn-suhn) did not bring enough food for the dogs. Instead, they planned to kill the most worn-out dogs during the trip.

The men tried to feed the meat from the dead dogs to the other dogs. But the Samoyed dogs refused to eat the meat. The dogs became hungry and tired. The men knew they would die without sled dogs. The team had to turn back before reaching the North Pole. Many dogs died during the trip. Only the strongest made it back alive.

Racing to the South Pole

Other explorers recognized the Samoyeds' talents as sled dogs. Robert Scott of England and Roald Amundsen (ROH-awld OM-uhnd-suhn) of Norway were Antarctic explorers. Both men wanted to be first to reach the South Pole. Both began their expeditions in 1911.

Scott's group had sleds with engines. These sleds were similar to snowmobiles. But the engines worked poorly and broke down. The men needed another way to reach the South Pole.

Scott also had dogs and ponies to pull sleds. The ponies came from Russia. They could survive in cold weather. Scott had sled dogs of different breeds. His dog team included 33 Samoyeds.

But Scott's group made a deadly mistake. They thought the dogs would do better with

Explorer Roald Amundsen of Norway wanted to be the first explorer to reach the South Pole.

their tails cut off. The explorers did not understand the importance of the dog's tail. The dog covers its nose with its tail when it sleeps. This keeps the dog's nose warm in cold weather. It also keeps cold air out of the dog's lungs. Scott's dogs caught pneumonia because they did not have tails to keep out the cold. They all died of this serious lung disease.

Scott's group kept going and had many difficulties. Their ponies could not make it across the ice. The ponies became sick and

Roald Amundsen arrived at the South Pole on December 14, 1911.

died. Scott and his men pulled their own sleds the rest of the way to the South Pole.

Scott's group reached the South Pole on January 18, 1912. But Scott's group did not know that Amundsen had already reached the Pole. Scott's group found dog tracks and a Norwegian flag. They were tired, sick, and upset that Amundsen had reached the South Pole first. Scott and his group never made it back to England. They all died on the return trip to their camp.

Amundsen's group was successful. The five men left for the South Pole with four sleds and 52 dogs. A team of 13 dogs pulled each sled. Amundsen's lead dog was a Samoyed named Etah (EE-tuh). Other Samoyed dogs also were part of his team. It took nearly two months to reach the Pole. The team arrived at the South Pole on December 14, 1911. Amundsen, his men, and 11 dogs made it home alive.

Many sled dogs became pets when they returned from the expeditions. These sled dogs were important to the Samoyed breed. They were the ancestors of Samoyeds today. These relatives from nearly 100 years ago passed on their strength and loyalty. Samoyeds are now famous for these traits.

Chapter 4
The Samoyed Today

Samoyeds were introduced in North America by Princess de Montyglyon (mon-te-GLEE-on). She was a Belgian countess in Europe. The brother of Czar Nicholas II of Russia had given her a Samoyed as a gift. The princess and her dog moved to the United States in 1904. This dog was the first Samoyed in North America.

People first registered Samoyeds with the American Kennel Club in 1906. Register means to record a dog's breeding record with an official club. The Samoyed Club of America began in 1923. Today, the American Kennel Club registers about 4,000 Samoyeds yearly.

In 1904, the first Samoyed arrived in North America.

The Canadian Kennel Club registers about 400 Samoyeds each year.

Sizing Up the Samoyed

Samoyeds are medium-sized dogs. But they make good sled dogs. Siberian Huskies are faster than Samoyeds. But Samoyeds are stronger than Siberian Huskies. Malamutes are stronger than Samoyeds. But Malamutes run slower than Samoyeds. Samoyeds can pull sleds with both strength and speed. Samoyeds are intelligent and friendly dogs. They work well with people.

Male Samoyeds are 21 to 23.5 inches (53 to 60 centimeters) tall. Females are 19 to 21 inches (48 to 53 centimeters) tall. People measure a dog's height from the ground to the withers. The withers are the tops of an animal's shoulders. Male Samoyeds weigh 45 to 65 pounds (20 to 29 kilograms). Females weigh 35 to 50 pounds (16 to 23 kilograms).

Samoyeds make good sled dogs because they are both strong and fast.

The Samoyed's Coat

Samoyeds have a thick, two-layer coat. The hairs of the outer layer are long and stiff. The Samoyed's outer hair is slightly oily. Water, snow, and dirt do not stick to the outer coat. This keeps the dog clean and dry.

A thick layer of soft, fluffy hair lies beneath the outer coat. The inner coat keeps the dog warm in winter. The Samoyed sheds its inner coat in warmer months. This keeps the dog cooler in summer. The Samoyed people collected the hair to make yarn. Today, some Samoyed owners still spin this hair into yarn.

All Samoyeds have light-colored coats. This hair can be pure white, cream, or biscuit. Biscuit is a very light tan. Most Samoyeds are all white. The outer coat has a silvery gleam at the tips. Many Samoyeds are white with biscuit coloring around the ears and eyes.

Samoyeds have extra-long hair around their necks and withers. These rings of hair are called ruffs. Males have more hair in their ruffs than females.

Sayomeds have extra-long hair around their necks and withers.

Chapter 5
Owning a Samoyed

Samoyeds are friendly. They enjoy people. Samoyeds do best when living with a family. They seem to like attention. They can become restless if left alone.

Samoyeds also need plenty of exercise to stay healthy. Owners should take walks with their Samoyeds. Then the dogs get attention and stay healthy.

Feeding and Care

Samoyeds have special health needs. Good food helps Samoyeds stay healthy. Quality dry dog food is best for a Samoyed. An adult Samoyed eats about 16 to 24 ounces

Samoyeds do best when living with a family.

(454 to 680 grams) of food a day. Dry foods made from rice, lamb, or chicken are healthiest. These foods give the dog everything it needs except water. Dogs need plenty of water. They should drink as often as they want. They need fresh water each day.

Samoyeds usually shed their thick coats in spring and late fall. They also shed some hair during the rest of the year. Owners should brush their Samoyeds every day. This helps keep the Samoyed clean. It also keeps dog hair from getting all over the house.

Hot weather can be hard on Samoyeds. They need air conditioning or cooler spots to rest in hot weather. Indoor areas such as basements or bare floors are cooler. Outdoors, Samoyeds sometimes dig a hole and lay on the dirt or find shade. This helps them stay cool.

Where to Get a Samoyed

A Samoyed club is a good place to find a Samoyed. Clubs have lists of breeders who raise and sell Samoyeds. Pet stores sometimes sell dogs that are not healthy. Good breeders

Samoyeds enjoy people and like attention.

try to raise healthy dogs. They understand the special needs of Samoyeds.

Owning a Samoyed requires some work. Samoyeds are active dogs that like to wander. They must be fenced in. They cannot be allowed to run free. Owners must train Samoyeds well. Samoyeds also need frequent grooming. But many people enjoy the loyalty and attention Samoyeds give. They think these dogs are worth the extra work.

Ears

Muzzle

Withers

Chest

Forequarters

Tail

Hindquarters

Hock

Quick Facts about Dogs

Dog Terms

A male dog is called a dog. A female dog is called a bitch. A young dog is called a puppy until it is 1 year old. A newborn puppy is called a whelp until it no longer needs its mother's milk. A family of puppies born at one time is called a litter.

Life History

Origin:	All dogs, wolves, coyotes, and dingoes descended from a single, wolf-like species. Humans trained dogs throughout history.
Types:	There are about 350 official dog breeds in the world. Dogs come in different sizes and colors. Adult dogs weigh from 2 pounds (1 kilogram) to more than 200 pounds (91 kilograms). They range from 6 inches (15 centimeters) to 36 inches (91 centimeters) tall.
Reproductive life:	Dogs mature at 6 to 18 months. Puppies are born two months after breeding. A female can have two litters per year. An average litter has three to six puppies. Litters of 15 or more puppies are possible.
Development:	Newborn puppies cannot see or hear. Their ears and eyes open one to two weeks after birth. Puppies try to walk when they are 2 weeks old. Their teeth begin to come in when they are about 3 weeks old.
Life span:	Dogs are fully grown at 2 years. They can live 15 years or longer with good care.

The Dog's Super Senses

Smell: Dogs have a strong sense of smell. It is
                many times stronger than a human's. Dogs
                use their nose more than their eyes and
                ears. They recognize people, animals, and
                objects just by smelling them. They may
                recognize smells from long distances. They
                also may remember smells for long periods
                of time.

Hearing: Dogs hear better than people do. Dogs can
                hear noises from long distances. They can
                also hear high-pitched sounds that people
                cannot hear.

Sight: Dogs' eyes are farther to the sides of their
                heads than people's are. They can see twice
                as wide around their heads as people can.

Touch: Dogs enjoy being petted more than almost
                any other animal. They also can feel
                vibrations from approaching trains or the
                beginning of earthquakes or storms.

Taste: Dogs do not have a strong sense of taste.
                This is partly because their sense of smell
                overpowers their sense of taste. It also is
                partly because they swallow food too
                quickly to taste it well.

Navigation: Dogs often can find their way home
                through crowded streets or across miles of
                wilderness without guidance. This is a
                special ability that scientists do not fully
                understand.

Words to Know

Bjelkier (BYEL-kyur)—the Samoyed people's name for the Samoyed dog; this name means "white dog that breeds white."

explorer (ek-SPLOR-ur)—a person who travels to foreign places to find out what they are like

lichen (LYE-ken)—a flat, mosslike growth on rocks and trees

Malamute (MA-luh-myoot)—a large sled dog from Alaska and northern Canada

pneumonia (noo-MOH-nyuh)—a serious lung disease that makes breathing difficult

reindeer moss (RAYN-dihr MAWSS)—a bushy, gray plant that grows in large patches in the Arctic; reindeer moss provides food for reindeer and other animals.

ruff (RUHF)—a ring of longer hair around an animal's neck and withers

To Learn More

American Kennel Club. *The Complete Dog Book for Kids*. New York: Howell Book House, 1996.

Rosen, Michael J. *Kids' Best Dog Book*. New York: Workman, 1993.

Rosen, Michael J. *Kids' Best Field Guide to Neighborhood Dogs*. New York: Workman, 1993.

Taylor, David. *Dogs*. New York: Dorling Kindersley, 1997.

Ward, Robert H., Dolly Ward and Mardee Ward-Fanning. *The New Samoyed*. New York: Howell Book House, 1998.

You can read articles about Samoyeds in *AKC Gazette*, *Dog Fancy*, *Dogs in Canada*, and *Dog World* magazines.

Useful Addresses

American Kennel Club
5580 Centerview Drive
Raleigh, NC 27606

Canadian Kennel Club
89 Skyway Avenue, Suite 100
Etobicoke, ON M9W 6R4
Canada

Organization for the Working Samoyed
1997 Big Owl Road
Allenspark, CO 80510

Samoyed Association of Canada
657 Valley Road
RR 3
Millbrook, ON L0A 1G0
Canada

Samoyed Club of America
3017 Oak Meadow Drive
Flower Mound, TX 75028

Internet Sites

American Kennel Club
http://www.akc.org

Canadian Kennel Club
http://www.canadiankennelclub.com

Dogs in Canada
http://www.dogsincanada.com

Organization for the Working Samoyed
http://www.samoyed.org/ows.html

Samoyed Association of Canada
http://www.samoyed.ca

Samoyed Club of America
http://www.samoyed.org

Samoyed Rescue
http://www.samoyed.org/samrescue.html

Index

Amundsen, Roald, 26–29
Antarctic, 26
Arctic, 5, 7, 9, 11, 15, 21, 25

Bjelkier, 17, 22
breeder, 38

coat, 34, 38
czar, 21, 22, 24, 31

England, 22, 23, 26, 29
Etah, 29
explorer, 21, 23, 25, 26
eyes, 5, 11, 12, 34

food, 9, 11, 15, 16, 19, 25, 37, 38

herd, 16, 18, 19

Johansen, Hjalmar, 25

Kilburn-Scott, Ernest, 22, 23, 24

Malamute, 33
moss, 8, 16, 19

Nansen, Fridtjof, 25–26
North Pole, 25, 26
Norway, 25, 26

pneumonia, 27
ponies, 26, 27

reindeer 5, 9, 16, 18–19
reindeer moss, 19
ruff, 34
Russia, 5, 7, 21, 22, 23, 24, 26, 31

Sabarka, 22
Samoyed Club, 23, 31
Samoyed people, 9, 11, 12–13, 15, 16, 17, 18, 19, 21, 22, 24, 34
Scott, Robert, 26, 27, 28, 29
sled, 5, 12, 16, 19, 21, 22, 23, 25, 26, 29, 33
South Pole, 26–29

tail, 5, 11, 27
Trontheim, Alexander, 22

water, 8, 34, 38